MW00474146

elemental
ALCHEMIST
GUIDED JOURNAL

ALSO BY **NYASHA WILLIAMS** AND **GRACE BANDA**

Elemental Alchemist Oracle Deck and Guidebook

NYASHA WILLIAMS AND **GRACE BANDA**

ILLUSTRATIONS BY **KIMISHKA NAIDOO**

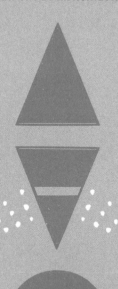

elemental
ALCHEMIST
GUIDED JOURNAL

Andrews McMeel
PUBLISHING®

ELEMENTAL ALCHEMIST copyright © 2023 by Nyasha Williams and Grace Banda. All rights reserved. Printed in China. No part of this book may be used or reproduced in any manner whatsoever without written permission except in the case of reprints in the context of reviews.

Andrews McMeel Publishing
a division of Andrews McMeel Universal
1130 Walnut Street, Kansas City, Missouri 64106

www.andrewsmcmeel.com

23 24 25 26 27 RLP 10 9 8 7 6 5 4 3 2 1

ISBN: 978-1-5248-8014-9

Editor: **DANYS MARES**
Art Director/Designer: **DIANE MARSH**
Production Editor: **MEG UTZ**
Production Manager: **TAMARA HAUS**

ATTENTION: SCHOOLS AND BUSINESSES
Andrews McMeel books are available at quantity discounts with bulk purchase for educational, business, or sales promotional use. For information, please email the Andrews McMeel Publishing Special Sales Department: sales@amuniversal.com.

contents

FROM GRACE

One of the very first ways I fell in love with writing was journaling. It is an amazing way to track growth and progress, mindfulness, and self-examination. For me, it was a magical place. No matter how I was feeling, it was there to capture my greatest and hardest emotions, and it was there to capture my beautiful stories. Getting to write this introduction is a great honor, and divination has been a strong part of acquiring all the knowledge needed for this. The creation of the *Elemental Alchemist Oracle Deck* aligned so perfectly with my spiritual awakening, and I got a great opportunity to write with my sister, Nyasha. I didn't think I had enough wisdom to write an oracle deck, but that's the thing about being called to something: Your ancestors and guides equip you with all you need. She saw the magic that I hadn't yet seen in myself, which motivated me to work on the shadows that I had ignored when all they needed was for me to love them for all of myself to begin healing. Becoming our best selves isn't easy, but having a book to journal, guide, and reflect on yourself is affirming.

I grew up in South Africa and struggled to truly connect to my culture, my roots, and my ancestors without really understanding why. Being well-read, well-spoken, and having access to travel was always one of the reasons I felt like an outcast among my own people. While none of these things are bad in any way, it is the conditioning of colonization that has caused our people to feel that way about ourselves and make each other feel like we are intellectually less than others. These cycles of generational trauma have existed for so long that they feel natural. It became easier just to accept that my culture and my roots didn't matter.

However, during my awakening and time away from home, I realized this was the intention of colonization—to lose ourselves. To reclaim our power within ourselves, within our indigenous ways, and within our ancestors and guides, we must decolonize. My sister has been a huge part of opening my eyes to that. Even though we have such different stories, we are connected as more than sisters: We are connected elementally.

In the same way, we have created this journal to connect you to the oracle deck as a divination tool and equip you with ways to channel the elements through your own life. The journey in this journal is the expansion of all you are made of, and may it be an inspiring tool to motivate courage, enlightenment, and growth.

Greatest wishes,

GRACE CB.

~autumn~

LAMMAS / LUGHNASADH / AUTUMN

NORTHERN HEMISPHERE: August 1

SOUTHERN HEMISPHERE: February 1

MABON / AUTUMN EQUINOX

NORTHERN HEMISPHERE: September 20–23

SOUTHERN HEMISPHERE: March 20–23

~summer~

BELTANE / SUMMER

NORTHERN HEMISPHERE: May 1

SOUTHERN HEMISPHERE: October 31–November 1

LITHA / SUMMER SOLSTICE

NORTHERN HEMISPHERE: June 20–23

SOUTHERN HEMISPHERE: December 20–23

OCTOBER

MABON

NOVEMBER

SAMHAIN

winter

DECEMBER

YULE

JANUARY

spring

IMBOLC

FEBRUARY

MARCH

winter

SAMHAIN / WINTER

NORTHERN HEMISPHERE: October 31

SOUTHERN HEMISPHERE: May 1

YULE / WINTER SOLSTICE

NORTHERN HEMISPHERE: December 20–23

SOUTHERN HEMISPHERE: June 20–23

spring

IMBOLC / SPRING

NORTHERN HEMISPHERE: February 1

SOUTHERN HEMISPHERE: August 1

OSTARA / SPRING EQUINOX

NORTHERN HEMISPHERE: March 20–23

SOUTHERN HEMISPHERE: September 20–23

wheel of the year

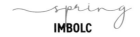

IMBOLC

NORTHERN HEMISPHERE: **February 1**

SOUTHERN HEMISPHERE: **August 1**

THEMES

- A fresh start
- Conception
- Creativity
- Inspiration
- Renewal, cleansing, and purification

ENERGY WORK

- Blessing
- Cleansing
- Fertility
- Luck
- Planting
- Protection
- Wishing

COLORS

- Pink
- Red
- White
- Yellow

PLANTS/HERBS

- Blackberry
- Chamomile
- Cinnamon
- Snowdrops
- Witch hazel

CRYSTALS

- Amethyst
- Bloodstone
- Citrine
- Turquoise

FOOD/DRINKS

- Oats
- Poppyseed cake
- Seeded bread
- Sunflower
- Pumpkin seeds

RITUALS

Time is potent with the rising energy of the Earth, and we can use this to bring forth our inner wisdom and inspiration to plant the seeds of our future growth. This is a season to continue the hibernation and restful days of winter while exploring our own inner landscapes and making plans for the future.

spring equinox
OSTARA

NORTHERN HEMISPHERE: March 20-23

SOUTHERN HEMISPHERE: September 20-23

THEMES

- Abundance
- Balance
- Cycles
- Fertility
- New life and beginnings

ENERGY WORK

- Balance
- Fertility
- Growth
- Renewal
- Sexuality

COLORS

- Green
- Pink
- White
- Yellow

PLANTS/HERBS

- Cleavers
- Clover
- Lemongrass
- Meadowsweet

CRYSTALS

- Amethyst
- Aquamarine
- Rose quartz

FOOD/DRINKS

- Eggs
- Honey
- Kale
- Lettuce
- Light breads
- Seeds
- Spinach

RITUALS

Rituals on this fire festival are typically centered around fertility and the celebration of life birthing anew. Spend this day involved in spring crafts that honor newborn life.

BELTANE

NORTHERN HEMISPHERE: **May 1**

SOUTHERN HEMISPHERE: **October 31–November 1**

THEMES

- Fertility
- Love
- Passion and sexuality

ENERGY WORK

- Creativity
- Fertility
- Love
- Prosperity
- Protection
- Sex

COLORS

- Red
- White
- Yellow

RITUALS

This day is often observed by crafting a crown of flowers, dancing around a bonfire, and delivering flowers and candles to loved ones for goodwill and community connection.

PLANTS/HERBS

- Daffodil
- Dandelion
- Hawthorne
- Meadowsweet
- Oak
- Paprika
- Primrose
- Rose

CRYSTALS

- Beryl
- Emerald
- Malachite
- Quartz
- Rose
- Sunstone

FOOD/DRINKS

- Cakes
- Elderflower
- Oats
- Sweet breads
- Wine

summer solstice

LITHA

NORTHERN HEMISPHERE: June 20-23

SOUTHERN HEMISPHERE: December 20-23

THEMES

- Abundance
- Joy
- Celebration
- Light
- Fulfillment

ENERGY WORK

- Happiness
- Luck
- Health
- Protection
- Love
- Relationships

COLORS

- Blue
- Green
- Gold
- Red

RITUALS

Rituals on this festival include staying up all night on midsummer's eve to welcome the sunrise, contemplating how you'd like to fortify your roots, and what you'd like to focus on internally during the dark season ahead.

PLANTS/HERBS

- Chamomile
- Rosemary
- Dandelion
- Sage
- Lavender
- St. John's wort
- Mint
- Sunflower
- Mugwort
- Thyme
- Mullein
- Verbena
- Rose

CRYSTALS

- Calcite
- Sunstone
- Citrine
- Yellow topaz
- Emerald

FOOD/DRINKS

- Apple cider
- Ice cream
- Carrots
- Squash
- Honey

LAMMAS / LUGHNASADH

THEMES

- Abundance
- Change
- Harvest
- Prosperity

ENERGY WORK

- Generosity
- Luck
- Prosperity

COLORS

- Bronze
- Green
- Orange
- Yellow

RITUALS

Celebrate Lammas, the harvest season, by hosting a feast full of seasonally available food.

PLANTS/HERB

- Basil
- Blackthorne
- Clover
- Ivy

CRYSTALS

- Amber
- Citrine
- Golden topaz
- Peridot
- Tiger's eye

FOOD/DRINKS

- Apples
- Bread
- Corn
- Honey
- Oats

autumn equinox
MABON

NORTHERN HEMISPHERE: September 20–23
SOUTHERN HEMISPHERE: March 20–23

THEMES

- Balance
- Fruitfulness
- Gratitude
- Harvest
- Rest

ENERGY WORK

- Balance
- Confidence
- Prosperity
- Protection
- Reflection

COLORS

- Bronze
- Brown
- Gold
- Green
- Orange
- Yellow

PLANTS/HERBS

- Chamomile
- Marigold
- Rosemary
- Sage

CRYSTALS

- Amber
- Citrine
- Lapis lazuli
- Quartz
- Sapphire

FOOD/DRINKS

- Apples
- Fresh meat
- Nuts
- Potatoes
- Wine

RITUALS

Celebrate Mabon by picking apples, baking apple pie, and creating an altar with symbols of the season, such as a cornucopia of autumn fruits and vegetables.

SAMHAIN

NORTHERN HEMISPHERE: October 31

SOUTHERN HEMISPHERE: May 1

THEMES

- Ancestors
- Death and rebirth
- Introspection
- Lifting the veil

ENERGY WORK

- Banishing
- Fairy magic
- Protection
- Release
- Spirit contact

COLORS

- Black
- Orange
- Purple

RITUALS

Spend this day honoring the ancestors who watch over you from the afterlife. On this day, the veil between worlds is thin, so it's a wonderful time to invite your deceased loved ones into your presence. Set a place for them at the table and serve them food to call them forward.

PLANTS/HERBS

- Calendula
- Garlic
- Nutmeg
- Rosemary
- Sage

CRYSTALS

- Bloodstone
- Clear Quartz
- Obsidian
- Onyx
- Smokey quartz

FOOD/DRINKS

- Apples
- Meat
- Parsnips
- Potatoes
- Pumpkin
- Spiced wine and cider

YULE

THEMES

- Hope after darkness and return of lights
- Introspection
- Transformation
- Rebirth

ENERGY WORK

- Happiness
- Peace
- Hope
- Strengthening bonds
- Love

COLORS

- Gold
- Silver
- Green
- White
- Red

PLANTS/HERBS

- Cinnamon
- Nutmeg
- Cloves
- Oak leaves
- Fir
- Pine

CRYSTALS

- Bloodstone
- Clear quartz
- Citrine
- Emerald

FOOD/DRINKS

- Hot cider
- Nuts
- Mulled wine
- Seasonal soups

RITUALS

Spend this day naming your intentions for the new year, looking outward, and bringing forth the lessons gained from the inner journey since the time of the summer solstice.

elemental COMMITMENT

Our current ways of life, rooted in the systems of colonization, systemic oppression, patriarchy, and capitalism, are toxic and unaligned with healthy, sustainable, and regenerative living for both ourselves and the planet as a whole. Decolonizing and indigenizing toward true liberation for all is the only way forward.

The cosmos, moon, Earth, continents, countries, water, and land are not objects to be exploited, abused, or drained as showcased by colonial action. We are in a living, breathing relationship with all creatures and land. Our relationship with these entities needs to reflect that.

As a world, we are disconnected from both ourselves and others. We must commit to consciously caring and nurturing our relationship with ourselves and with our community. Strengthening our disconnection from others is the idea of scarcity, which breeds competition and seeing others as oppositions to your success. Each one of us is enough, and our worth or value is not dictated by our production. There is more than enough for all of us to walk in abundance and move in creativity.

For our equitable world to become a reality, we need to make conscious choices in who we do business with and how we conduct our business to ensure they are regenerative, accountable, and responsible partnerships with others and the planet.

Are you living in alignment with the world you wish to see for future generations?

The elements are a major part of returning to ourselves and finding the balance we have been disconnected from.

It is time to unlearn white-supremacist culture and align with new agreements to rebuild our connection with ourselves, others, and the world, moving toward an equitable world for all. This means honoring the traditions and habits of some of our first Ancestors. They knew that there was no separation between us and the elements. They are all around and within us.

MANTRAS TOWARD DECOLONIZING

I COMMIT TO HONORING MY RELATIONSHIP WITH THE LAND,
WITH ALL WATER, AND ALL LIVING CREATURES,
AS THEY ARE NECESSARY FOR THE EXISTENCE OF LIFE.

I COMMIT TO NURTURING AND STRENGTHENING MY
RELATIONSHIP WITH MYSELF AND WITH OTHERS, KNOWING
OUR DESTINIES AND PROGRESS ARE INTERTWINED.

I COMMIT TO KNOWING THAT I AM ENOUGH AND BELIEVING
IN THE ENOUGHNESS AND VALUE OF OTHERS.

I COMMIT TO LIVING, BUILDING, AND CREATING IN WAYS THAT SUPPORT,
UPLIFT, AND NOURISH ALL BEINGS AND THE ENVIRONMENT.

LAYOUT

THE JOURNAL IS DIVIDED INTO FIVE SECTIONS OF THREE WEEKS, EACH SECTION FOCUSING ON A DIFFERENT ELEMENT. EACH ELEMENT HAS BULLET TRACKERS FOR THE TIME SPENT IN THE SECTION, AN ACTIVITY, A SHADOW WORK PROMPT, AND AN ORACLE READING RECORDER FOR EACH WEEK.

BULLET TRACKERS

Because establishing and sticking to a routine can sometimes be overwhelming and stifling, we created trackers aimed at helping you build a ritualistic living around habits that will bring comfort as they are flexible in what they can look like to each individual. The trackers aid in you being present and developing a ritualist way of living.

The trackers are coloring pages for you to creatively note your rituals and routines.

◯ FILL MY CUP

The systems that we currently live in aren't serving us as a community and do not encourage rest or self-care. Nurturing our health (spiritual, emotional, mental, and physical) into elemental balance needs to become a daily practice. Our world does not reward listening to our bodies or making space for a natural balance. This is your sign to shed the Gregorian calendar, to begin living with the seasons and slowing your pace when you hear the call, just as nature and our Ancestors did. The Fill My Cup tracker is a reminder to regularly practice filling up your cup and giving to others from the overflow.

> SELF-CARE SUGGESTIONS FOR EACH ELEMENT (SELF-CARE MENUS) ARE AVAILABLE IN EACH SECTION.

○ MAGICAL HOUSEKEEPING

Spiritual cleaning and cleansing are just as important as the physical hygiene of our bodies, hair, and clothes. Our energetic selves and spaces need to be cared for and reset. In our technology-heavy and the information-overloaded world, imbalances or excess energy are common, disrupting your natural flow.

Protecting one's energy and spaces energetically is essential, and the tracker works to help make the tasks regular practice.

> ALWAYS OPEN UP ALL OF THE WINDOWS IN YOUR SPACE WHEN DOING MAGICAL HOUSEKEEPING OR CLEANSING.

When cleansing or cleaning, do each task with focused intent; that's where the magic comes in. Speak what you want over yourself and your space for your highest good and ease.

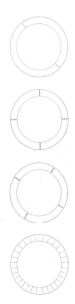

~daily
CLEANSING - SELF + SPACE

WAYS OF CLEANSING:
- Smoke (sweet grass, cedar, rosemary, mugwort, juniper, lavender, frankincense, myrrh)
- Salt and lemon bowl
- Water (spiritual bath, creating a spiritual mist to spray around the space in a spray bottle)
- Sound (sound bowls, binaural beats, bells)
- Crystals

~weekly
CLEANSING - SPACE

WAYS OF CLEANSING:
- Vinegar (for surfaces, pour down all parts of plumbing)
- Floor wash (sweep, normal floor washing, and then a magical floor wash)
- Wiping down walls (use a magical wash)
- Doing washing (bedding or clothes—add Florida water to each load)
- Water on Altar (replace)

~biweekly
CLEANING - ALTAR

(take care of the space in which you connect with spirit)

WAYS OF CLEANSING YOUR ALTAR:
- Changing the water on your Altar
- Removing offerings that are not fresh anymore
- Changing the clothes on your Altar

◯ MEDITATION

Meditation doesn't have to look a particular way. Meditation should allow your motivation to increase, bring about a night of better sleep, lower your stress levels, and enhance mental clarity.

Meditation should bring about heightened awareness and relaxation. Listen to what calls to you in terms of traditional and nontraditional forms of meditation.

MEDITATION:

- Body scan
- Breath awareness
- Focus
- Loving-kindness
- Mantra
- Mindfulness
- Transcendental

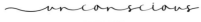

MEDITATION:

- Art/crafting
- Building
- Gardening
- Walking

◯ GRATITUDE

The world and our day-to-day lives can get extremely difficult from time to time.

**MAKING SPACE FOR GRATITUDE
HELPS US TO REMEMBER THAT
NOT ALL IS LOST, AND OUR FLOW
OF PEACE WILL RETURN.**

Staying in gratitude is not always easy when you care for our world and others deeply. We all have work to do here down on Earth to better the world for future generations. If our focus is only on what is going wrong and what needs to be fixed, it makes it difficult to dream anew and function at our best for building the world we believe in. Remember, you are your Ancestors' dreams come true. Your rest, joy, and peace are revolutionary.

The gratitude tracker is a space to track all the good that you are experiencing and, if you are ever feeling stumped in finding something to be grateful for, use the elements as your guide.

ACTIVITIES

Each elemental section has one activity for each week toward connecting you with that specific element. Like a muscle, the activities exercise your mind and energetically balance you out.

The three activities in the journal are an elemental observation, a meditation, and a deeper connecting activity. The observational activity is to observe and record the specific element in its most natural form. Your meditations can be recorded in the meditation tracker along with any other forms of meditation you feel called to. The connecting activity is to get you to build a more personal connection with said element.

SHADOW WORK

Shadow work is working to bring forth the unconscious parts of yourself and parts of yourself that have been abandoned and denied in an attempt to be accepted or loved. Shadow work is the walk toward healing yourself. Returning to yourself is a huge part of our spiritual journey here on earth. Understand that returning to our highest selves means returning to the truest you. The you that felt safe, loved, and engaged with the world from your heart. The you that wasn't dulled or dimmed to meet societal expectations or standards. The you that believed and loved to dream. Our job is to heal back into that self, our whole self.

TO START SEEING YOUR SHADOW SELF:

• View your emotional triggers as lessons, showing you what and/or where you need to heal.
• Notice when you judge, blame, or criticize.
• Work through the journal prompts honestly and thoroughly.

SIGNS OF GROWTH AND HEALING THROUGH SHADOW WORK:

- Abundance
- Authentic living
- Being present
- Compassion
- Discovering your soul mission
- Grounded
- Patience
- Peace
- Revolutionary optimism
- Secure boundaries
- Self-love
- Trust

ORACLE READING

Use these spreads to record your oracle readings while focusing on each element and working through each section of the journal. Take note of your thoughts surrounding the reading. The recordings will allow you to track patterns, cycles, growth, and what comes to manifest. Allow your observations to help you gain a deeper understanding of yourself.

THE FIVE
elements

THE ESSENCE OF LIFE IS COMPOSED OF THE FIVE ELEMENTS: SPIRIT, AIR, FIRE, EARTH, AND WATER. SPIRIT, THE ONLY NONPHYSICAL ELEMENT, FLOWS WITHIN ALL THE OTHER ELEMENTS. EACH ELEMENT HELPS US BETTER UNDERSTAND THE ALIGNMENTS, ABILITIES, AND CONNECTIONS OF WHAT OUR LIVES ARE COMPOSED OF AND HOW ELEMENTS NOURISH US. BY UNDERSTANDING EACH ELEMENT'S POSITIVE AND NEGATIVE ASPECTS, WE CAN ALIGN OURSELVES BY USING AND HONORING EACH ELEMENT MOST EFFECTIVELY.

ELEMENTAL ANATOMY

When any element in your body is out of balance, your wellness is affected physically and emotionally. Elemental anatomy of the body is just as essential to learn as scientific human anatomy. All five elements are a part of different structures in your body. The two most dominant elements in the body are water and earth.

- **WATER** (approximately 72 percent of your body composition) shapes your fluids: blood, saliva, sweat, urine, etc.

- **EARTH** (approximately 12 percent of your body composition) shapes your physical frame: skin, muscles, bones, tissues, hair, and nails.

- **AIR** (approximately 6 percent of your body composition) shapes your movement: gross and fine motor skills, muscle contraction, gas expansion, and suppression.

- **FIRE** (approximately 4 percent of your body composition) shapes your bodily replenishment: sleep, thirst, hunger, and human connection.

- **SPIRIT** (approximately 6 percent of your body composition) shapes your thoughts and feelings: fear, happiness, attraction, personality, and ego.

Remember that this is only the elemental anatomy—how the elements physically make up your human body. As you learn more about them, you will find that the elements represent different things spiritually, which can help heal your physical anatomical body and the spirit flowing through it.

ELEMENTAL RELATIONSHIPS

Based on the characteristics of the various elements, each element will connect and form relationships distinctively. Think about yourself and all the people in your life, how different they all are, and how that affects your relationship with them. Elements were the first bond, the first relationship that formed the laws of nature.

ELEMENTAL LOVE: These elements encourage and support each other's growth by flowing into each other to create. (Earth & Water) (Fire & Air)

ELEMENTAL COOPERATION: These elements are amicable and can cooperate without any problems; however, after their partnership has served its purpose, they separate. (Water & Air) (Earth & Fire) (Air & Earth)

ELEMENTAL ENEMIES: These elements need to be separate to coexist; too much of one destroys the other, and equally, they destroy each other. (Fire & Water)

spirit

SPIRIT IS UNIVERSAL ENERGY BECAUSE, WITHOUT SPIRIT, NONE OF THE OTHER FOUR ELEMENTS CAN EXIST. IT EXISTS WITHIN US, ABOVE US, AND BELOW US. THAT IS WHY WE MUST EXPRESS GRATITUDE DAILY FOR THE SPIRIT. FOR GIVING US THE ELEMENTS, GIVING OUR SOULS LIFE, A UNIVERSAL CONNECTION TO OUR ANCESTORS TO FORM DEEPER CONNECTIONS, AND SUPPORTING, SYNCHRONIZING, AND UNITING ALL LIFE FORMS.

WHEN YOU EXPERIENCE AN AWAKENING, SPIRIT HELPS YOU BETTER ALIGN UNIVERSAL ENERGY WITH YOUR OWN. A NEW AWARENESS OF THE WORLD COMES WITH SPIRIT, BUT NOT WITHOUT SELF-TRANSFORMATION. THERE IS A REASON GREAT POWER REQUIRES GREAT RESPONSIBILITY. THE MORE YOU WANT TO CONNECT WITH THE SPIRITUAL ELEMENT, THE MORE SELF-WORK, DECOLONIZATION, AND APPRECIATION MUST BE EXPRESSED.

SPIRIT CORRESPONDENCES

DIRECTION: Central (Within/Without)
GENDER: All Genders, Genderless
TIME OF DAY: All-Time, Eternal
SEASON: All Seasons, All Movement
PLANET: Sun

ALTAR OBJECTS OF SPIRIT

- Pictures of Ancestors, Deities, or anyone you feel connected to spiritually
- Crystals (clear quartz, danburite, petalite, spodumene, amethyst)
- Any representation of the Elements
- Candles

oracle

MONTHLY TRACKER

S	M	T	W	T	F	S
◯	◯	◯	◯	◯	◯	◯
◯	◯	◯	◯	◯	◯	◯
◯	◯	◯	◯	◯	◯	◯
◯	◯	◯	◯	◯	◯	◯
◯	◯	◯	◯	◯	◯	◯

key

- ◯ _____
- ◯ _____
- ◯ _____
- ◯ _____
- ◯ _____
- ◯ _____
- ◯ _____
- ◯ _____
- ◯ _____
- ◯ _____
- ◯ _____
- ◯ _____
- ◯ _____
- ◯ _____

- ◯ _____
- ◯ _____
- ◯ _____
- ◯ _____
- ◯ _____
- ◯ _____
- ◯ _____
- ◯ _____
- ◯ _____
- ◯ _____
- ◯ _____
- ◯ _____
- ◯ _____
- ◯ _____

fill my cup
TRACKER

key

1. _____

2. _____

3. _____

4. _____

5. _____

6. _____

7. _____

8. _____

9. _____

10. _____

11. _____

12. _____

13. _____

14. _____

15. _____

16. _____

17. _____

18. _____

19. _____

20. _____

21. _____

ALTAR CLEANING

CHANGE WATER ON ALTAR

magical housekeeping
TRACKER

CLEANSING SELF + SPACE

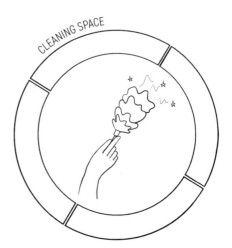

CLEANING SPACE

gratitude
TRACKER

key

1. _____

2. _____

3. _____

4. _____

5. _____

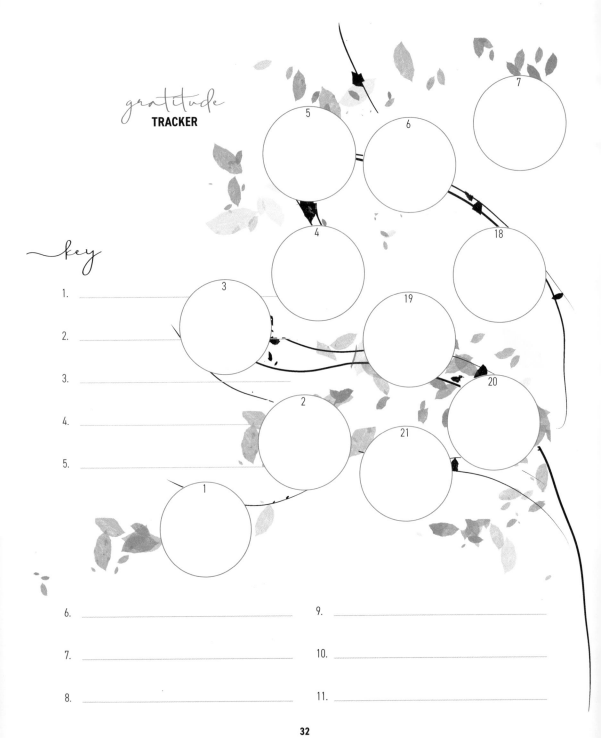

6. _____   9. _____

7. _____   10. _____

8. _____   11. _____

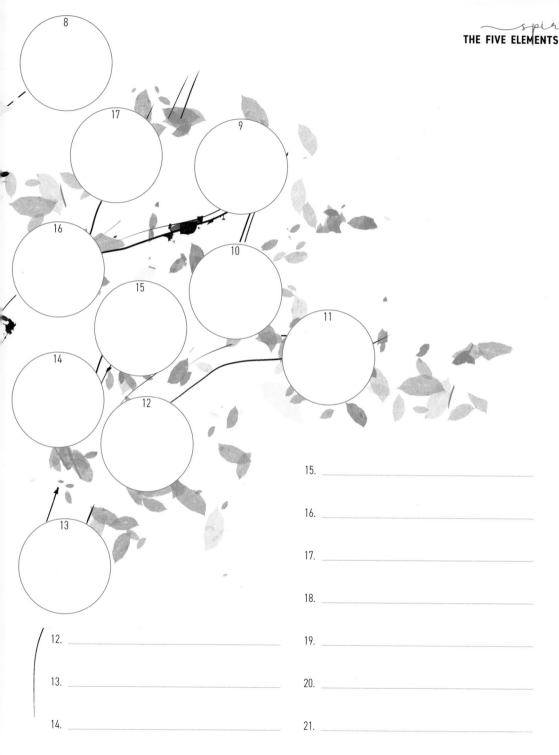

15. _____

16. _____

17. _____

18. _____

19. _____

20. _____

21. _____

12. _____

13. _____

14. _____

ELEMENTAL OBSERVATION
dream awareness

Dreams carry messages, but oftentimes, we forget them as soon as we wake up. Getting into the habit of dream journaling helps us better remember them and tune in to what our spirits and minds need. For three consecutive nights, record your dreams in this section right after you wake up. No matter how much or how little you remember, just write what you can. Keep in mind that not all your dreams will make sense or relate to you.

example

DATE: January 1, 2022

DREAM TITLE: The River

ASSOCIATED ELEMENTS/ATMOSPHERE/WEATHER/LOCATION: Water and Earth, Near a riverbank

DREAM SYMBOLS: Fast moving water flow, white clothes

INTERPRETATION: My ancestors are with me; the white makes it easier for us to communicate. New beginnings are coming. Healing is beginning, but I shouldn't be afraid. The current will take me where I need to be.

HOW I FELT IN MY DREAM: Calm, but fearful of falling into the water even though it is where I am meant to be.

HOW I FEEL NOW: Optimistic

OTHER SIGNIFICANT DETAILS: In the background, I heard a big African drum almost calling me to the water in joy.

day one

DATE:

DREAM TITLE:

ASSOCIATED ELEMENTS/ATMOSPHERE/WEATHER/LOCATION:

DREAM SYMBOLS:

INTERPRETATION:

HOW I FELT IN MY DREAM:

HOW I FEEL NOW:

OTHER SIGNIFICANT DETAILS:

DATE:

DREAM TITLE:

ASSOCIATED ELEMENTS/ATMOSPHERE/WEATHER/LOCATION:

DREAM SYMBOLS:

INTERPRETATION:

HOW I FELT IN MY DREAM:

HOW I FEEL NOW:

OTHER SIGNIFICANT DETAILS:

day three

DATE:

DREAM TITLE:

ASSOCIATED ELEMENTS/ATMOSPHERE/WEATHER/LOCATION:

DREAM SYMBOLS:

INTERPRETATION:

HOW I FELT IN MY DREAM:

HOW I FEEL NOW:

OTHER SIGNIFICANT DETAILS:

shadow work
PROMPT

ARE YOU ABLE TO ASK OTHERS FOR FORGIVENESS?

ARE YOU ABLE TO FORGIVE OTHERS?

READING

DATE: _____

S   M   T   W   T   F   S

MOON PHASE: _____

SPREAD TITLE: _____

QUESTION(S): _____

CARD(S) PULLED:

INTUITIVE UNDERSTANDING:

DEEPER INSIGHTS:

ACTION TO TAKE AFTER READING:

DAY SUMMARY AND THOUGHTS REFLECTING ON READING LATER:

SPIRIT MEDITATION

awaken your spirit body awareness

This meditation is best done with spirit element/aether/space binaural beats, but you are more than welcome to meditate in silence.

This spiritual guided meditation helps you access and strengthen the loving connection between your body and spirit. You may find yourself feeling almost as though you're floating during this practice, and you may never view your body the same again!

• Begin this meditation by lying flat on your back, palms at your sides facing up. Leave some space between your legs, allowing your feet to fan outward. Make any adjustments you need to accommodate your comfort in this position. Once your body feels nice and relaxed, close your eyes and begin to allow yourself to pull your awareness inward, tuning in to your breath and your body. Feel your belly rise at every inhale and fall on every exhale. Allow the air to travel freely without restriction, letting the breath be whatever it wants to be. Let all the muscles in your body relax. Explore the idea of what your breath does for your body.

• As you explore what happens on every breath that is flowing through your body, you will recognize that you are acknowledging your own physical form as conscious and wise, functioning with its own natural intelligence. Appreciate your breath for teaching you this lesson.

• With every breath, every cell, every atom your spirit lives and it unites with the physical mechanisms of your body, bringing love and consciousness. Let yourself relax for a few breaths as you feel what this truth feels like within you.

• As you relax more deeply into this spirit-body connection, you will also become aware of this loving, nonphysical energy all around you. You recognize that, even if only for these moments, your own consciousness, your own spirit, as vast and infinite, cocreating with this beautiful physical form that emanates and loves unconditionally. Relax into this loving connection, feeling the spirit and body, united through love. Feel spirits' intention for your physical form, feel how the intention is all-loving. Stay connected to this feeling and intention as you take your time coming back to the world around you. Stretch your arms and legs as you feel called, wiggling fingers and toes, moving slowly, really feeling your body. Your body and spirit are connected as you move. Whenever you are ready, open your eyes.

• Enjoy the rest of your day, connected to this vision.

PROMPT

WHERE DO YOU FEEL THE EXPECTATION TO CONFORM TO THE BELIEFS OF OTHERS?

WHERE DO YOU EXPECT OTHERS TO CONFORM TO YOUR BELIEFS?

READING

DATE:

S   M   T   W   T   F   S

MOON PHASE:

SPREAD TITLE:

QUESTION(S):

CARD(S) PULLED:

INTUITIVE UNDERSTANDING:

DEEPER INSIGHTS:

ACTION TO TAKE AFTER READING:

DAY SUMMARY AND THOUGHTS REFLECTING ON READING LATER:

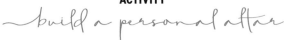

This is a highly personal project that will help connect you with your spiritual side and honor your resilience.

1. Intention/Purpose of the Altar

What will your altar be used for? Spiritual or personal practices? This can be for self-love, for those you have lost, for journaling, and for wisdom. The purpose of your altar is entirely what feels needed to you.

2. Choose a Space for Your Altar

Pick a place where your altar will not be easily disturbed and where there will be a good energetic flow. Go with what feels right to you.

3. Cleanse the Space

Cleanse the area in any way you feel called to cleanse. This can be smudging, spraying spiritual waters, and so much more.

4. Acquire Tools/Objects for Your Altar

Use your intuition to collect any tools and objects that you would like to keep on your altar. Remember to include tools and objects that are elemental to help balance your altar energetically.

5. Arrange Your Altar

Once the altar space has been cleansed and tools gathered, you can arrange and place your tools on your altar. Don't overthink the placement of anything, simply let it resonate with you and what feels right to you. You can always rearrange when you feel called to move something.

6. Work With and Maintain Your Altar (Cleaning & Connecting)

Once everything is set up, be sure to regularly cleanse and find ways to connect with your altar.

PORTABLE ALTAR
(DISCREET AND PORTABLE ALTERNATIVE)

Sometimes finding a good place for an altar can be hard when you don't have the space or are always moving around and traveling. You can make a portable altar instead.

Choose an intention, and find a container (box, tin candy container, etc.) of whatever size you want your portable altar to be. Acquire tools and objects that will fit your container and arrange your items. Once you are done, store your altar close to you.

shadow work
PROMPT

DO YOU FEEL LOVED, HEARD, AND VALUED BY YOURSELF? BY OTHERS IN YOUR LIFE?

READING

DATE:

S   M   T   W   T   F   S

MOON PHASE:

SPREAD TITLE:

QUESTION(S):

CARD(S) PULLED:

INTUITIVE UNDERSTANDING:

_____
_____
_____
_____
_____
_____
_____

DEEPER INSIGHTS:

_____
_____
_____
_____
_____
_____
_____

ACTION TO TAKE AFTER READING:

_____
_____
_____
_____
_____
_____
_____

DAY SUMMARY AND THOUGHTS REFLECTING ON READING LATER:

_____
_____
_____
_____
_____

air

AIR IS OUR MOST BASIC CONNECTION TO LIFE—ONE OF THE VERY FIRST ELEMENTS OUR BODIES MAKE CONTACT WITH AFTER BIRTH. IT SYMBOLIZES NEW BEGINNINGS, HIGHER CONSCIOUSNESS, COMMUNICATION, INTELLECT, AND THOUGHT. AS AN ELEMENT OF THE MIND, AIR SHIFTS OUR WORLD INTO ACTION AND COGNIZANCE WITH ITS SWIFT-MOVING NATURE. WHAT AIR CHANGES AND REMOVES FROM OUR PATHS IS IMPERATIVE FOR EXPANSION.

WHEN IN BALANCE, AIR CALMS AND TEMPERS THE MIND. HOWEVER, WHEN LACKING AIR, IT CAN BE HARD TO SEE THINGS OBJECTIVELY, AND WHEN OVERACTIVE, IT HOLDS THE CAPACITY TO CLOUD YOUR MIND WITH DISCONNECTION, ANXIETY, AND IMPULSIVITY.

AIR CORRESPONDENCES

DIRECTION: East

GENDER: Masculine

ASTROLOGICAL SIGNS: Aquarius (January 20–February 9), Gemini (May 21–June 20), Libra (September 23–October 22)

TIME OF DAY: Dawn

SEASON: Spring

MOON PHASE: Waning Moon

ALTAR OBJECTS OF AIR

- Smoke incense/diffuser
- Crystals (clear quartz, citrine, smoky quartz/topaz)
- Feather
- Bell orwindchimes
- Musical instrument
- Athame or swords

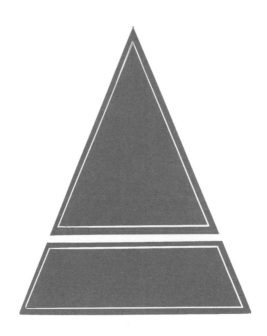

oracle

MONTHLY TRACKER

S	M	T	W	T	F	S
◯	◯	◯	◯	◯	◯	◯
◯	◯	◯	◯	◯	◯	◯
◯	◯	◯	◯	◯	◯	◯
◯	◯	◯	◯	◯	◯	◯
◯	◯	◯	◯	◯	◯	◯

key

○ _____   ○ _____

○ _____   ○ _____

○ _____   ○ _____

○ _____   ○ _____

○ _____   ○ _____

○ _____   ○ _____

○ _____   ○ _____

○ _____   ○ _____

○ _____   ○ _____

○ _____   ○ _____

○ _____   ○ _____

○ _____   ○ _____

○ _____   ○ _____

○ _____   ○ _____

○ _____   ○ _____

fill my cup
TRACKER

key

1. _____

2. _____

3. _____

4. _____

5. _____

6. _____

7. _____

8. _____

9. _____

10. _____

11. _____

12. _____

13. _____

14. _____

15. _____

16. _____

17. _____

18. _____

19. _____

20. _____

21. _____

ALTAR CLEANING

CHANGE WATER ON ALTAR

magical housekeeping
TRACKER

CLEANSING SELF + SPACE

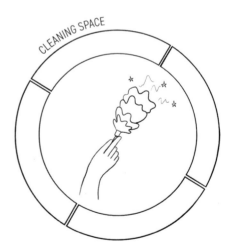

CLEANING SPACE

meditation
TRACKER

gratitude **TRACKER**

key

1. _____
2. _____
3. _____
4. _____
5. _____
6. _____
7. _____
8. _____
9. _____
10. _____
11. _____

12. _____
13. _____
14. _____
15. _____
16. _____
17. _____
18. _____
19. _____
20. _____
21. _____

ELEMENTAL OBSERVATION

sky gazing

The clouds move and become what they are because of air's interaction with water and heat. Cloud gazing promotes imagination, creativity, calmness, while helping you to focus on the element of air.

Take some time on three different occasions (which can be spread out through the week or consecutively) to watch clouds in the sky and write down your observations. Write at least a couple of sentences each time, observing the texture and color of the clouds, what you think they feel like, how the air is moving them, what shapes they are forming, etc. Feel free to take pictures, draw, or do anything you feel called to do to add to your elemental observation.

ENTRY ONE

ENTRY TWO

ENTRY THREE

shadow work
PROMPT

HOW GOOD ARE YOU AT SHOWING YOURSELF COMPASSION, GRACE, AND UNDERSTANDING?

HOW GOOD ARE YOU AT SHOWING OTHERS COMPASSION, GRACE, AND UNDERSTANDING?

READING

DATE: _____

S   M   T   W   T   F   S

MOON PHASE: _____

SPREAD TITLE: _____

_____

_____

QUESTION(S): _____

_____

_____

CARD(S) PULLED:

INTUITIVE UNDERSTANDING:

DEEPER INSIGHTS:

ACTION TO TAKE AFTER READING:

DAY SUMMARY AND THOUGHTS REFLECTING ON READING LATER:

AIR MEDITATION
breathwork

Take a few moments to sit comfortably, ideally with your back straight and with the soles of your feet on the floor, as we begin with three minutes of focusing on our breathing. Set an intention for new beginnings, movement, or communication.

BREATHE IN, BREATHE OUT.
NO SPACE BETWEEN THE
INHALE AND EXHALE.

KEEP THAT FLOWING. If you need to pause for a second, that is okay. We are looking to do this for three minutes.

MINUTE ONE: We start to fill ourselves up with oxygen, spreading it to every cell of our body. After a minute, if you want to take a pause, take a pause. Feel alive. Become aware of what it is like to be more oxygenated. Oxygen is the fountain of your life and existence.

MINUTE TWO: Let's start breathing again; breathing in and breathing out. The constant flow of oxygen spreading into every cell of your body. From your nose to your toes, from your toes to your hands, from your hands to your heart, from your head and all through your body as you continue to allow oxygen to flow.

MINUTE THREE: Again, breathe in and breathe out. Allowing yourself to feel great, to feel alive, to be in the present moment. Beautiful. If your mind wanders that is fine, just bring it back. You are incredible.

• Now take a moment to think about three different times in your life where you felt gratitude. Open up the memories one by one and let the energy of each flow through and all around you.

• Gradually slow down your breathing and come back to yourself.

shadow work
PROMPT

ARE THERE PARTS OF YOUR AUTHENTIC SELF THAT YOU MASK?

WHAT ARE YOUR REASONS FOR MASKING?

oracle

READING

DATE: _____

S   M   T   W   T   F   S

MOON PHASE: _____

SPREAD TITLE: _____
_____
_____

QUESTION(S): _____
_____
_____

CARD(S) PULLED:

INTUITIVE UNDERSTANDING:

DEEPER INSIGHTS:

ACTION TO TAKE AFTER READING:

DAY SUMMARY AND THOUGHTS REFLECTING ON READING LATER:

ACTIVITY

design a daily routine

CREATE A ROUTINE IN YOUR DAYS THAT ENCOURAGES STABILITY, CALMNESS, AND
PEACE. IN YOUR CAPTURE, WRITE YOUR DAY AS A STORY.

shadow work
PROMPT

WHERE ARE YOU ON YOUR SELF-LOVE JOURNEY?

DO YOU LOVE ALL OF YOURSELF UNCONDITIONALLY?

READING

DATE: _____

S   M   T   W   T   F   S

MOON PHASE: _____

SPREAD TITLE: _____

_____

_____

QUESTION(S): _____

_____

_____

CARD(S) PULLED:

INTUITIVE UNDERSTANDING:

DEEPER INSIGHTS:

ACTION TO TAKE AFTER READING:

DAY SUMMARY AND THOUGHTS REFLECTING ON READING LATER:

fire

FIRE IS THE DRIVING FORCE BEHIND ALL LIFE PROCESSES, THE ELEMENT OF ABSOLUTE LIGHT, INTENSITY, AND HEAT. IT SYMBOLIZES COURAGE, PASSION, PURIFICATION, WILL, AND RENEWAL. AS THE ELEMENT OF ZEAL, FIRE IS THE CONDUIT FOR ACTING ON WHAT MAKES YOU FEEL ALIVE AND IS KNOWN AS THE UNIVERSAL ENERGY BECAUSE THE SUN IS AN INITIATOR FOR ALL CREATION. WHAT IS DESTROYED IN THE FIRE IS INVOKED TO CLEANSE YOU IN FIRE AND GET YOU READY FOR NEW CREATION.

WHEN IN BALANCE, FIRE CAN HELP BURN THROUGH INSECURITY AND NEGATIVITY, OFTEN ALSO ACTING AS A CATALYST FOR OTHERS. HOWEVER, WHEN LACKING FIRE, ONE CAN BECOME UNINSPIRED AND STAGNANT AND SEE NO POINT IN ANYTHING. WHEN OVERACTIVE, IT HOLDS THE CAPACITY TO CLOUD YOU WITH CARELESSNESS, GREED, AND INCONSIDERATION AND BURN YOU OUT. IT SHOULD BE NOTED THAT FIRE IS THE HARDEST OF THE ELEMENTS TO BALANCE BECAUSE IT IS THE ONE THAT MAKES US FEEL THE MOST ALIVE.

FIRE CORRESPONDENCES

DIRECTION: South

GENDER: Masculine

ASTROLOGICAL SIGNS: Aries (March 21–April 19), Leo (July 23–August 22), Sagittarius (November 22–December 21)

DAY OF THE WEEK: Sunday and Tuesday

TIME OF DAY: Noon

SEASON: Summer

MOON PHASE: Waxing Moon

ALTAR OBJECTS OF FIRE

- Flame (candle, lamp, or brazier)
- Crystals (ruby, carnelian, amber, opal)
- Cactus or thorns
- Lighter or matches
- Smudging
- Wands

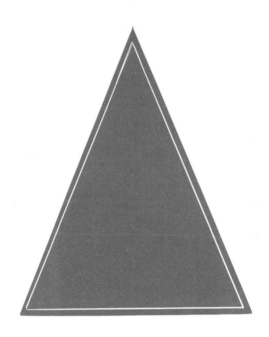

oracle

MONTHLY TRACKER

S	M	T	W	T	F	S
○	○	○	○	○	○	○
○	○	○	○	○	○	○
○	○	○	○	○	○	○
○	○	○	○	○	○	○
○	○	○	○	○	○	○

key

- ○ _____
- ○ _____
- ○ _____
- ○ _____
- ○ _____
- ○ _____
- ○ _____
- ○ _____
- ○ _____
- ○ _____
- ○ _____
- ○ _____
- ○ _____
- ○ _____
- ○ _____

- ○ _____
- ○ _____
- ○ _____
- ○ _____
- ○ _____
- ○ _____
- ○ _____
- ○ _____
- ○ _____
- ○ _____
- ○ _____
- ○ _____
- ○ _____
- ○ _____

8 9 10 11 12 13 14

1 2 3 4 5 6 7

15 16 17 18 19 20 21

fill my cup
TRACKER

key

1. _____

2. _____

3. _____

4. _____

5. _____

6. _____

7. _____

8. _____

9. _____

10. _____

11. _____

12. _____

13. _____

14. _____

15. _____

16. _____

17. _____

18. _____

19. _____

20. _____

21. _____

ALTAR CLEANING

CHANGE WATER ON ALTAR

magical housekeeping
TRACKER

CLEANSING SELF + SPACE

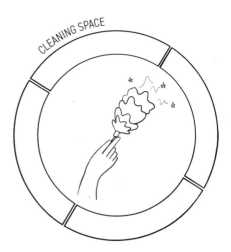

CLEANING SPACE

meditation
TRACKER

1   2   5   7   9   12 13

21   14

20   3   4   15

                 6   8   10   11   16

19   17

18

gratitude
TRACKER

key

1. _____

2. _____

3. _____

4. _____

5. _____

6. _____

7. _____

8. _____

9. _____

10. _____

11. _____

12. _____

13. _____

14. _____

15. _____

16. _____

17. _____

18. _____

19. _____

20. _____

21. _____

ELEMENTAL OBSERVATION

working with candles

Place some candles in your space, whatever kind you feel called to. Take some time to observe the health of your candle over three entries (just a couple lines each time or one for each candle). Candles can tell you so much about the energy of your space. The way the flame interacts with the wick and the wax, the way the air feeds the fire, how big or small the flame is. Feel free to take pictures, draw, or do anything you feel called to do to add to your elemental observation.

ENTRY ONE

ENTRY TWO

ENTRY THREE

shadow work
PROMPT

DO YOU BELIEVE INTENT MATTERS MORE THAN IMPACT OR IMPACT MORE THAN INTENT?

oracle

READING

DATE: _____

S   M   T   W   T   F   S

MOON PHASE: _____

SPREAD TITLE:

_____

_____

_____

QUESTION(S):

_____

_____

_____

CARD(S) PULLED:

INTUITIVE UNDERSTANDING:

_____
_____
_____
_____
_____
_____
_____

DEEPER INSIGHTS:

_____
_____
_____
_____
_____
_____

ACTION TO TAKE AFTER READING:

_____
_____
_____
_____
_____
_____

DAY SUMMARY AND THOUGHTS REFLECTING ON READING LATER:

_____
_____
_____
_____

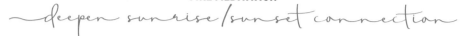
FIRE MEDITATION

deepen sunrise/sunset connection

Consciousness and connection to the sun's movements are vital for our physical, emotional, and mental health. These sunrise/sunset meditations will help you greet the beginning and end of your day.

SUNRISE MEDITATION

Sit in a comfortable seated position or lie down. Begin to focus on your breath. As the room fills with the light of the sun, imagine what you'd like to leave behind in the darkness of the night. What thoughts, feelings, or habits are no longer serving you? What parts of yourself and your life do you want to shed light on today? When the sun has risen and the room is filled with light, send gratitude to the rays for the life they provide.

SUNSET MEDITATION

Find a quiet place outdoors or in a room with windows and either close your eyes or keep them open and watch the light change. Get comfortable and begin to focus on the breath. As the room darkens, feel your mind get quiet. Feel the chaos of your day melting off of you. Release the negative and the positive and allow the sunset to dissolve anything you might be holding on to and anything that you don't want to carry into the night. What do you offer up to the night? What can you release?

PROMPT

WHAT'S THE ONE THING YOU KNOW YOU NEED TO DO BUT KEEP AVOIDING?

WRITE IT DOWN. THEN WRITE A STEP-BY-STEP DESCRIPTION OF ACTUALLY DOING IT.

INCLUDE EVERY ACTION REQUIRED IN ORDER TO GET IT DONE.

READING

DATE: _____

S   M   T   W   T   F   S

MOON PHASE: _____

SPREAD TITLE:
_____
_____
_____

QUESTION(S):
_____
_____
_____

CARD(S) PULLED:

INTUITIVE UNDERSTANDING:

_____
_____
_____
_____
_____
_____
_____
_____

DEEPER INSIGHTS:

_____
_____
_____
_____
_____
_____

ACTION TO TAKE AFTER READING:

_____
_____
_____
_____
_____
_____

DAY SUMMARY AND THOUGHTS REFLECTING ON READING LATER:

_____
_____
_____
_____
_____

ACTIVITY

cook yourself a hot meal

For millions of years the element of fire has been used to transform food. This doesn't go for all cooking, but heat is a large part of many cuisines. It kills harmful bacteria that may cause food poisoning or simply makes a meal taste more appealing.

The act of making that which will nourish you, and taking the time to feed your body, is a form of self-care. All of your senses are engaged when cooking: smell, taste, touch, sight, and sound. They all form a powerful memory imprint. That is why eating foods from your childhood can be so nostalgic. So take some time to cook for yourself and/or others and record the recipe.

recipe

SERVES:

PREP TIME:

COOK TIME:

TOTAL TIME:

CUISINE:

INGREDIENTS

-
-
-
-
-
-
-
-
-
-
-

DIRECTIONS

recipe

SERVES:

PREP TIME:

COOK TIME:

TOTAL TIME:

CUISINE:

INGREDIENTS

-
-
-
-
-
-
-
-
-
-
-
-
-
-
-
-
-
-
-

DIRECTIONS

shadow work
PROMPT

DESCRIBE YOUR INNER CHILD.

WRITE DOWN THE WAYS YOU HONOR OR WOULD LIKE TO HONOR YOUR INNER CHILD.

READING

DATE: _____

| S | M | T | W | T | F | S |

MOON PHASE: _____

SPREAD TITLE: _____

_____

_____

QUESTION(S): _____

_____

_____

CARD(S) PULLED:

INTUITIVE UNDERSTANDING:

_____
_____
_____
_____
_____
_____
_____

DEEPER INSIGHTS:

_____
_____
_____
_____
_____
_____

ACTION TO TAKE AFTER READING:

_____
_____
_____
_____
_____
_____

DAY SUMMARY AND THOUGHTS REFLECTING ON READING LATER:

_____
_____
_____
_____

earth

EARTH IS THE MOST POWERFUL OF ALL ELEMENTS, IT GIVES US OUR BIRTH ALONGSIDE WATER. WHILE WE LIVE, IT NOURISHES US, AND WHEN WE DIE, IT ALLOWS US TO BECOME PART OF IT. IT SYMBOLIZES STABILITY, GROUNDING, CYCLES, HEALTH, HEARTH, AND WISDOM. AS THE ELEMENT OF STABILITY, EARTH CARRIES ADAPTABILITY AND CREATIVITY, WHICH ENCOURAGES THE WORLD TO GROW AND EXPAND. AND JUST LIKE ANY GARDEN, THE SOIL MUST BE READY BEFORE PLANTING.

WHEN IN BALANCE, THE EARTH HARMONIZES AND STRENGTHENS THE MIND, MAKING ROOM FOR GOALS. HOWEVER, WHEN LACKING EARTH, IT CAN BE HARD TO SET GOOD BOUNDARIES, ACCEPT SELF-LOVE, AND ACCEPT CHANGE. WHEN OVERACTIVE, IT HOLDS THE CAPACITY TO CLOUD YOUR MIND WITH ANXIETY, MATERIALISM, AND STRESS.

EARTH CORRESPONDENCES

DIRECTION: North

GENDER: Feminine

ASTROLOGICAL SIGNS: Taurus (April 20–May 20), Virgo (August 23–September 22), Capricorn (December 22–January 19)

DAY OF THE WEEK: Thursday and Saturday

TIME OF DAY: Midnight

SEASON: Winter

MOON PHASE: New Moon

ALTAR OBJECTS OF EARTH

- The altar (base) itself
- Crystals (garnet, hematite, jasper, aventurine)
- Flowers, herbs, or seeds
- Food offerings (especially fruits, vegetables, or grain foods)
- Rocks or stones
- Coins

oracle

MONTHLY TRACKER

S	M	T	W	T	F	S
◯	◯	◯	◯	◯	◯	◯
◯	◯	◯	◯	◯	◯	◯
◯	◯	◯	◯	◯	◯	◯
◯	◯	◯	◯	◯	◯	◯
◯	◯	◯	◯	◯	◯	◯

key

○ _____   ○ _____

○ _____   ○ _____

○ _____   ○ _____

○ _____   ○ _____

○ _____   ○ _____

○ _____   ○ _____

○ _____   ○ _____

○ _____   ○ _____

○ _____   ○ _____

○ _____   ○ _____

○ _____   ○ _____

○ _____   ○ _____

○ _____   ○ _____

○ _____   ○ _____

○ _____   ○ _____

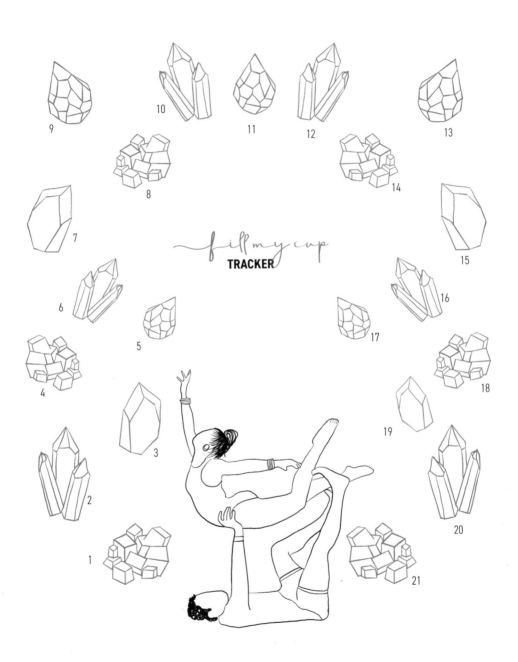

fill my cup
TRACKER

9
10
11
12
13
8
14
7
15
6
16
5
17
4
18
3
19
2
20
1
21

key

1. _____

2. _____

3. _____

4. _____

5. _____

6. _____

7. _____

8. _____

9. _____

10. _____

11. _____

12. _____

13. _____

14. _____

15. _____

16. _____

17. _____

18. _____

19. _____

20. _____

21. _____

ALTAR CLEANING

CHANGE WATER ON ALTAR

magical housekeeping
TRACKER

CLEANSING SELF + SPACE

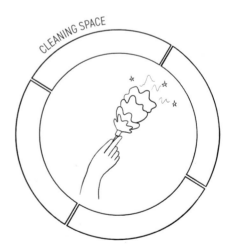

CLEANING SPACE

meditation
TRACKER

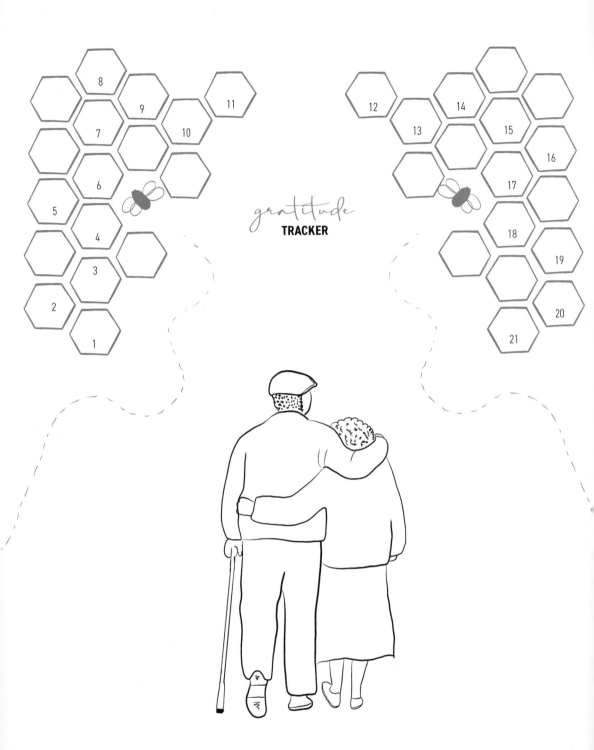

gratitude
TRACKER

8
9
11
7
10
6
5
4
3
2
1

12
14
13
15
16
17
18
19
20
21

key

1. _____

2. _____

3. _____

4. _____

5. _____

6. _____

7. _____

8. _____

9. _____

10. _____

11. _____

12. _____

13. _____

14. _____

15. _____

16. _____

17. _____

18. _____

19. _____

20. _____

21. _____

ELEMENTAL OBSERVATION

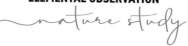

Spend one hour in nature three days out of the week (which can be spread out through the week or taken consecutively) and journal about how you feel in nature. Write at least three to five sentences each time, observing the seasonal changes, sitting at the roots of plants, feeling plants, observing animals, etc. Feel free to take pictures, draw, or do anything you feel called to add to your nature study.

ENTRY ONE

ENTRY TWO

ENTRY THREE

shadow work

PROMPT

IF YOU COULD WRITE A LETTER TO SOMEONE WHO HAS HURT YOU, WHAT WOULD IT SAY?

READING

DATE: _____

S   M   T   W   T   F   S

MOON PHASE: _____

SPREAD TITLE: _____

_____

_____

QUESTION(S): _____

_____

_____

CARD(S) PULLED:

INTUITIVE UNDERSTANDING:

DEEPER INSIGHTS:

ACTION TO TAKE AFTER READING:

DAY SUMMARY AND THOUGHTS REFLECTING ON READING LATER:

EARTH MEDITATION
grounding yourself

Whenever you are feeling like you're spinning out, things are moving too quickly, or there's too much activity for you to be able to focus, take a few moments to do this guided visualization to help you ground into a place of safety, security, and solidity.

- Begin by finding a comfortable seat and focus your breathing on slow, deep inhalations and exhalations.

- Imagine a white light coming directly from a source above and bring that energy down into your physical body through the crown of your head.

- Next, imagine that energy moving directly down your spine and out through the soles of your feet all the way down into the center of the Earth.

- See, imagine, or feel any energetic imbalances within you being moved down and out through your feet directly into the earth to be recycled. Ask that any imbalances be washed away.

- Now bring the pure, solid, reliable, grounding energy of Earth—and all that she represents to you—back up through your feet and up your legs, stopping at the top of your legs just below the hips.

- Allow yourself to feel the qualities of earth that you most need to draw upon at this time: permanence, reliability, safety, security—whatever it is that you need at this moment.

- When you feel the sensation of the earth qualities you most need to experience at this moment, affirm to yourself that you can access this feeling anytime you need to by simply taking the time to connect to the element of earth in this way.

- Open your eyes slowly, jot down any notes or thoughts that you felt were important, and go on about your day.

shadow work

PROMPT

DESCRIBE YOUR DREAM/ULTIMATE/HIGHEST SELF.

ARE THERE THINGS HOLDING YOU BACK FROM BECOMING THAT PART OF YOU?

oracle

READING

DATE: _____

S   M   T   W   T   F   S

MOON PHASE: _____

SPREAD TITLE: _____
_____
_____

QUESTION(S): _____
_____
_____

CARD(S) PULLED:

INTUITIVE UNDERSTANDING:

DEEPER INSIGHTS:

ACTION TO TAKE AFTER READING:

DAY SUMMARY AND THOUGHTS REFLECTING ON READING LATER:

ACTIVITY

draw yourself as a tree

YOUR ROOTS WILL BE LOADED WITH DESCRIPTIONS OF THINGS THAT GIVE YOU STRENGTH AND YOUR GOOD QUALITIES, WHILE YOUR LEAVES CAN BE THE THINGS THAT YOU'RE TRYING TO CHANGE.

shadow work
PROMPT

WHAT IS ONE THING THAT YOU WISH TO CHANGE ABOUT SOCIETY?

HOW WOULD THIS WISH COMING TRUE AFFECT OTHERS AND YOURSELF?

READING

DATE: _____

| S | M | T | W | T | F | S |

MOON PHASE: _____

SPREAD TITLE: _____
_____
_____

QUESTION(S): _____
_____
_____

CARD(S) PULLED:

INTUITIVE UNDERSTANDING:

_____
_____
_____
_____
_____
_____
_____

DEEPER INSIGHTS:

_____
_____
_____
_____
_____
_____

ACTION TO TAKE AFTER READING:

_____
_____
_____
_____
_____
_____

DAY SUMMARY AND THOUGHTS REFLECTING ON READING LATER:

_____
_____
_____
_____
_____

water

THE WATER ELEMENT IS A HUGE LIFE FORCE, THE MOST PRESENT ELEMENT IN BOTH OUR BODIES AND THE EARTH. IT SYMBOLIZES SPIRITUALITY, EMOTION, INTUITION, AND CLEANSING. AS THE ELEMENT OF FLOW, WATER CAN APPEAR GENTLE, LIKE PROTECTING LIFE IN THE WOMB, BUT CARRIES THE IMMENSE POWER TO DESTROY, LIKE A HURRICANE. NO MATTER THE FLOW, WATER DEMANDS TO WASH OVER ALL YOUR EMOTIONS.

WHEN IN BALANCE, WATER PULLS OUT NEGATIVITY AND PROVIDES HEALING AND TRANQUILITY. HOWEVER, WHEN LACKING, HARSHNESS TOWARD YOURSELF AND OTHERS COMES EASILY, AS WELL AS DESENSITIZATION FROM EMOTIONS AND EMPATHY. WHEN OVERACTIVE, IT CAN BE HARD TO SEE ANYTHING CLEARLY WITHOUT ALL THE INTENSE EMOTIONS OR HEAVY BAGGAGE ATTACHED TO IT, MAKING IT HARD TO LET GO OF THINGS THAT NO LONGER SERVE YOU.

WATER CORRESPONDENCES

DIRECTION: West

GENDER: Feminine

ASTROLOGICAL SIGNS: Pisces (February 19–March 20), Cancer (June 22–July 22), Scorpio (October 23–November 21)

DAY OF THE WEEK: Monday and Friday

TIME OF DAY: Dusk

SEASON: Autumn

MOON PHASE: Full Moon

ALTAR OBJECTS OF WATER

- Seashells
- Crystals (aquamarine, lapis lazuli, sodalite, amethyst)
- Mirror or scrying bowl
- Beverages (especially water but also libations)
- Rainwater
- Chalice, cup, or goblet

oracle

MONTHLY TRACKER

S	M	T	W	T	F	S
◯	◯	◯	◯	◯	◯	◯
◯	◯	◯	◯	◯	◯	◯
◯	◯	◯	◯	◯	◯	◯
◯	◯	◯	◯	◯	◯	◯
◯	◯	◯	◯	◯	◯	◯

key

- ○ _____
- ○ _____
- ○ _____
- ○ _____
- ○ _____
- ○ _____
- ○ _____
- ○ _____
- ○ _____
- ○ _____
- ○ _____
- ○ _____
- ○ _____
- ○ _____
- ○ _____

- ○ _____
- ○ _____
- ○ _____
- ○ _____
- ○ _____
- ○ _____
- ○ _____
- ○ _____
- ○ _____
- ○ _____
- ○ _____
- ○ _____
- ○ _____
- ○ _____
- ○ _____

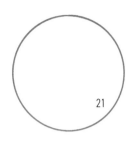

21

fill my cup
TRACKER

11

10

9

8

7

6

5

4

3

2

1

12

13

14

15

16

17

18

19

20

key

1. _____

2. _____

3. _____

4. _____

5. _____

6. _____

7. _____

8. _____

9. _____

10. _____

11. _____

12. _____

13. _____

14. _____

15. _____

16. _____

17. _____

18. _____

19. _____

20. _____

21. _____

ALTAR CLEANING

CHANGE WATER ON ALTAR

magical housekeeping
TRACKER

CLEANSING SELF + SPACE

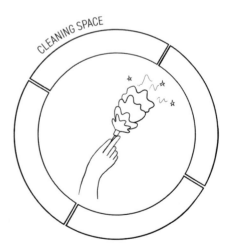

CLEANING SPACE

meditation
TRACKER

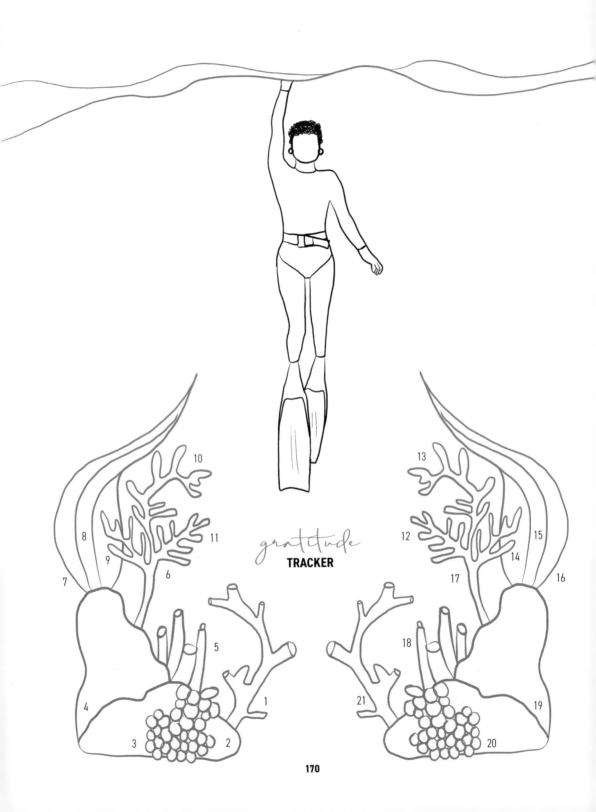

gratitude
TRACKER

key

1. _____

2. _____

3. _____

4. _____

5. _____

6. _____

7. _____

8. _____

9. _____

10. _____

11. _____

12. _____

13. _____

14. _____

15. _____

16. _____

17. _____

18. _____

19. _____

20. _____

21. _____

ELEMENTAL OBSERVATION

charging your water

In the same way we send energy to what we want to manifest or we sleep to recharge our bodies, we should give energy to anything going inside our bodies. Take time to express affirmation and/or gratitude to the water that gives you life and nourishes and sustains you. Journal about how you feel about the interaction of water. Write at least three to five sentences each time you drink water about how refreshed and hydrated you feel, observing your body's response to the water.

Feel free to add to your elemental observation energetically, like adding water-safe crystals to your water, steeping tea/herbs, sunlight charging, and/or moonlight charging.

ENTRY ONE

_____
_____
_____
_____
_____

ENTRY TWO

_____
_____
_____
_____
_____

ENTRY THREE

_____
_____
_____
_____
_____

PROMPT

HOW DO YOU CURRENTLY HONOR THE ENVIRONMENTS YOU ARE A PART OF?

WHAT COULD YOU DO TO MAKE THEM BETTER?

READING

DATE: _____

S   M   T   W   T   F   S

MOON PHASE: _____

SPREAD TITLE: _____
_____
_____

QUESTION(S): _____
_____
_____

CARD(S) PULLED:

INTUITIVE UNDERSTANDING:

_____
_____
_____
_____
_____
_____
_____

DEEPER INSIGHTS:

_____
_____
_____
_____
_____
_____

ACTION TO TAKE AFTER READING:

_____
_____
_____
_____
_____
_____

DAY SUMMARY AND THOUGHTS REFLECTING ON READING LATER:

_____
_____
_____
_____
_____

WATER MEDITATION

intuitive connection

This meditation is best done while in a body of water or observing water while listening to water or binaural beats.

• Let go . . . Let go of all your thoughts. See a waterfall of mystical energy pour down on the top of your head and cascade down your body, purifying and cleansing you. Washing away your past, washing away your pain. It is crystal clear, beautiful water; notice the color and shimmer as the light dances among the droplets. It washes away all that no longer serves you down into the earth to be recycled and renewed.

• This cleansing water begins to penetrate and absorb into your physical body. Your body and the water become one. Feel the steady free flow and the peaceful sensation that comes with letting go. You and the water are one body, you begin to flow from the base of the waterfall, down a beautiful river. Flowing over rocks and obstacles with such ease, unstoppable, powerful, and free. This river washes into an ocean and this ocean touches all large bodies of water across the Earth. Enjoy being stretched across the Earth in these bodies of water. Notice how you feel being extended and connected across the Earth in water.

• You are in complete alignment with true freedom, surrendering to the flow of the current. The ocean supports you and is so happy that you are connecting with it. The ocean has many gifts to share with you; take a deep breath and be open to the healing and wisdom of the ocean and all it has to share with you at this time.

• You invite the compassionate spirit of the sea to come forth and connect with you. They swim toward you. Notice how they move, the color, texture, and feeling you get as they approach you. This compassionate being has a message just for you. Allow it to share its message with words, movements, or feelings.

• The spirit of water would like you to merge with them or hold on to them to take you and your soul to shore. As you approach the shoreline of the sandy beach, let go of this compassionate spirit. Offer water appreciation for their time and connection in any way that feels best to you.

- You then begin to swim to shore but realize as you approach your legs have formed a magical, beautiful tail. You are now a merperson (mermaid, merman, merfolk). As you swim, notice the magnificent colors of your scales and how the light reflects off of them. You are in shallow waters now, enjoying the feeling of being a being of the sea. Colorful, tropical fish are drawn to you and your beautiful tail, they being to swim around you.

- You are now surrounded by every spectrum of the rainbow offered by your tail, the fish, and coral reef beneath you. These colors swirl around you, filling you with the healing energy of the chakra colors. Filling your energy field with all that it needs at this time.

- You shed your scales, and your legs and feet appear beneath them. However, your skin has absorbed all the colors. Begin to exit the water and meditation, saying goodbye to the ocean and the fish and thanking them for their colors.

- Slowly return to your body with a nice deep breath. You are magical, you are radiant, you are loved . . . Now shine your light into the world.

shadow work
PROMPT

LOOKING FORWARD FIVE YEARS FROM NOW, WHERE DO YOU WANT TO BE, WHAT DO YOU WANT TO BE DOING, AND WHAT DOES YOUR LIFE LOOK LIKE?

WHAT DOES THE WORLD LOOK LIKE?

READING

DATE: _____

S   M   T   W   T   F   S

MOON PHASE: _____

SPREAD TITLE: _____
_____
_____

QUESTION(S): _____
_____
_____

CARD(S) PULLED:

INTUITIVE UNDERSTANDING:

_____
_____
_____
_____
_____
_____
_____
_____

DEEPER INSIGHTS:

_____
_____
_____
_____
_____
_____
_____

ACTION TO TAKE AFTER READING:

_____
_____
_____
_____
_____
_____
_____

DAY SUMMARY AND THOUGHTS REFLECTING ON READING LATER:

_____
_____
_____
_____
_____

ACTIVITY
spiritual bath

Spiritual baths are great for cleansing your energy, clearing your mind, and magical inner healing. Take some time to yourself and connect with water more deeply.

There is no incorrect way to take a spiritual bath; however, there are still efforts that need to be put into the bath for it to vibrate higher. Each bath is prepared and set to your intention and needs. If you need a guide, below are tips to create a great spiritual bath experience.

• Take a shower before soaking, since this will clean you, and the intent of the bath will be strictly to relax and clear the blockages.

• Make sure that the tub you are using is clean and relaxing. Make the bathroom your sacred space for this time. Light some candles and burn some aromatherapy oils and/or incense.

• Decide on the intention of the bath. The energy you give to this bath is what you will get back.

• Fill the tub with clean water and add ingredients that match your intention. It could be salt, milk, flowers, body and spiritual oils, etc.

• You can choose to be in silence or have meditation or relaxing sounds playing.

• Spend twenty to thirty minutes in your spiritual bath.

• Dispose of any ingredients from your bath outside your house.

• Take some time to rest and wind down.

IF YOU DON'T HAVE A BATHTUB, YOU CAN STILL DO A SPIRITUAL BATH, JUST WITH A LITTLE MORE CREATIVITY. INSTEAD OF BATHING IN A TUB, YOU CAN PUT YOUR INGREDIENTS ON YOUR SHOWER FLOOR AND STEAM, OR MAKE IT IN THE SINK AND POUR THE WATER OVER YOU, STARTING FROM THE CROWN OF YOUR HEAD AND WORKING DOWNWARD. DISPOSE OF THE INGREDIENTS IN THE SAME WAY, AND RELAX.

shadow work
PROMPT

WHAT GIVES TO YOU ENERGETICALLY AND WHAT TAKES FROM YOU ENERGETICALLY?

READING

DATE: _____

S   M   T   W   T   F   S

MOON PHASE: _____

SPREAD TITLE: _____

_____

_____

QUESTION(S): _____

_____

_____

CARD(S) PULLED:

INTUITIVE UNDERSTANDING:

_____
_____
_____
_____
_____
_____
_____

DEEPER INSIGHTS:

_____
_____
_____
_____
_____
_____
_____

ACTION TO TAKE AFTER READING:

_____
_____
_____
_____
_____
_____
_____

DAY SUMMARY AND THOUGHTS REFLECTING ON READING LATER:

_____
_____
_____
_____
_____

oracle deck
SPREADS

elements of life
SPREAD

1. **SPIRIT:** Representing your true self

2. **AIR:** Representing clarity on what you need most right now

3. **EARTH:** Representing your environment, internal and external

4. **WATER:** Representing how you communicate

5. **FIRE:** Representing manifestations

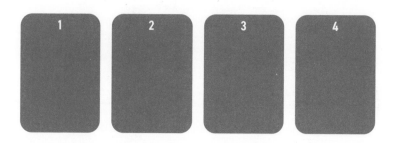

spirit
SPREAD

1. The state of your connection to spirit

2. What is limiting the connection

3. How can you tune in to your intuition

4. What you need to add to your physical
    life to strengthen your inner self

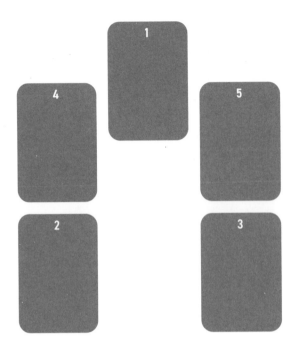

SPREAD

1. The current state of your thoughts

2. Problems that may prevent you from focusing on your intentions

3. Your state of flexibility around change

4. What you can do to remove cloudiness that will give you clarity

5. How you should welcome changes

fire
SPREAD

1. The desires and passions you have for life

2. What is holding you back from achieving those desires

3. The spark you need to create the life you want

4. How to embrace growth after these desires come to pass

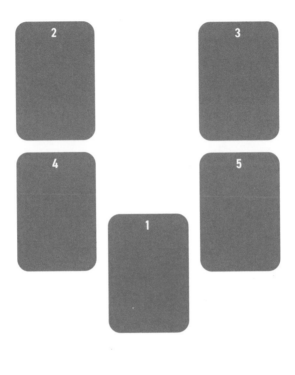

earth

SPREAD

1. Current state of your roots

2. The reason you are not grounded

3. What you need to do to become grounded

4. What you need add to your daily life to build a relationship with the earth and your grounded self

5. The state of your mountain—how you grow after you reach the peak

water

SPREAD

1. The state of your emotions in this moment

2. What is preventing your emotions from flowing

3. What you need to release to restore fluidity

4. What positive habits you need to adopt, mentally and/or physically

5. Outcome of your emotional release

ABOUT THE
~ authors

NYASHA WILLIAMS, a passionate social justice griot, grew up living intermittently between the United States and South Africa. Nyasha's mission is to use words and stories to decolonize literature, minds, and spiritual practices.

Nyasha is a firm believer that the story lives within each of us and that it is our mission to use stories to spread understanding, healing, and empowerment. Nyasha encourages us to uncover and share our stories through her work so that we can all learn, grow, and create meaningful change.

Nyasha's writing is rooted in her understanding of the powerful potential of stories to create transformation and reveal truths that have been hidden for too long. She strives to use her words to ignite new conversations, inspire action, and ultimately help create a more equitable and just world.

"As BIPOCs, we are operating and navigating systems that weren't made for us and are actively working against us," says Williams. "My efforts as a creator, author, and activist are to combat the systems of White supremacy, colonization, and the patriarchy, working towards decolonizing, liberating, and indigenizing our minds and world."

Writing to Change the Narrative is Nyasha's way of bringing her passion for storytelling to life and helping us all to write our own stories. With her help, we can all find our voices and use them to write a better world.

Her latest children's book, *Ally Baby Can: Be Feminist,* was just released, and she has five additional children's book titles coming out in 2023. She has a tarot deck, *Black Tarot: An Ancestral Awakening Deck and Guidebook,* that came out in December 2022. You can find her on Instagram at @writingtochangethenarrative. She lives in Northglenn, Colorado, with her husband.

GRACE BANDA is a South African storyteller and herbalist who understands the power of stories in her culture and hopes to craft meaningful tales that can recreate and reimagine a new world.

Grace has never lost her love of stories. She grew up surrounded by Gauteng's vibrant culture and energy, and she's used those experiences to fuel her imagination and create stories that share her passion for her homeland. She believes in the power of story to shape the way we see the world, and she's been on a mission to use her voice to make a difference.

A quote that resonates with her is Audre Lorde's, "I have come to believe over and over again that what is most important to me must be spoken, made verbal and shared, even at the risk of having it bruised or misunderstood."

Because all voices are important, and everyone's story deserves to be heard, not silenced.

In addition to her writing and storytelling, Grace is also an avid herbalist and student of indigenous herbalism. She loves exploring plants' healing power and sharing her knowledge with others.

She hopes to continue sharing her work, stories, and herbalism with the world.

ABOUT THE
illustrator

KIMISHKA NAIDOO is a proud South African woman of South Asian descent. With a passion for celebrating cultures, Kimishka was raised to embrace the duality of her identity and to appreciate other cultures from a young age.

The creative talent in Kimishka has led her to study film, video editing, animation, graphics design, and teaching English as a second language. She has also been fortunate enough to travel throughout Europe and Asia giving her the opportunity to learn more about the unique cultures that reside there.

Building on her cultural appreciation and creative background, Kimishka has begun to express her creativity through illustrations that highlight and amplify her appreciation for BIPOC culture and beauty.

Kimishka's mission is to encourage people to embrace the beauty of different cultures, celebrate the beauty of inclusivity, and empower people to be proud of their roots. Kimishka is a driving force for positive change, and her art is her way of sharing her message of love and acceptance with the world.